TEACHING THINKING SKILLS
in the
PRIMARY YEARS

A Whole School Approach

by
Michael Pohl

HAWKER BROWNLOW
E D U C A T I O N

Dedication

This book is dedicated to all
the problem solvers of the future.
May they employ their thinking
abilities wisely in making the world
a safe and prosperous place for everyone.

Acknowledgements

It is difficult to identify everyone who has contributed directly or indirectly in bringing this book into reality.

To those who seeded the idea, sensed the need and encouraged me to persevere - I thank you.

Thanks also, to all the teachers who trialled the modules and provided the invaluable feedback to ensure that this book would meet their needs and the needs of others.

I would also like to sincerely thank Debbie Draper for allowing me to use the teaching and learning activities that appear in module six.

Lastly, I wish to acknowledge the support and contribution of my wife, Karen. This book would not have been written without her support, encouragement and proofreading skills.

Contents

Foreword

Few people concerned with the education of young minds would argue that one of the primary objectives of schooling should involve the teaching of tools for life-long learning.

When asked to list important tools for life-long learning, many educators would place a high priority on empowering students with thinking skills such as the ability to reason; to make informed judgements; to critically evaluate information and to think creatively.

As a consultant visiting dozens of schools and talking with hundreds of teachers, it became increasingly obvious to me that whilst they had clearly articulated guidelines and policies for just about everything remotely connected to student learning - the teaching of thinking skills across the school was a common exception.

The purpose of this book is to fill that void - by giving teachers a manageable framework for the explicit teaching of thinking skills which will equip students with thinking tools to use throughout their schooling and in the years beyond.

Used as intended, these modules provide a scope for the teaching of thinking in the primary grades that encompasses a wide range of strategies, many of which are aimed at developing higher order thinking skills.

More importantly, this book provides the framework for **a whole school approach** to the explicit teaching of thinking skills across the primary grades. The modules can easily be sequenced so that students may be exposed to (and hopefully master) the diversity of thinking strategies presented in this book before they move into secondary schools.

Samples of activities that will assist in determining whether learning outcomes have been achieved have been included. Teachers may also choose to record student progress on the proformas to be found near the end of each module.

Teachers will be familiar with most tools and strategies outlined in the modules and so only brief explanations of each strategy have been provided. More detailed information and further examples for how to use each tool can be found in the selected reference list provided at the end of each module.

Introduction

Why a whole school approach?

It is not uncommon to hear teachers in schools talking about developing a *thinking culture* within their learning communities.

In developing a thinking culture, it will be important to provide teaching and learning activities that will

- empower students with the language, tools and strategies to engage in a wide range of analytical, critical and creative thinking tasks

- provide on-going opportunities for developing, practising and refining the skills of thinking

- provide instruction and practice in ways of managing, organising and recording thinking

- engage students (particularly the more gifted learners) in the higher order thinking skills

- assist in the transfer of skills to everyday life and everyday situations as tools for life-long learning.

Achieving such outcomes will require more than the efforts of a few teachers occasionally using one or two thinking strategies as a part of their normal classroom practice.

> An essential element in developing a thinking culture will be the explicit teaching of thinking skills to all students.

A whole-school approach that provides a scope and sequence for the introduction of thinking skills at specific year levels will have a much greater chance of success in achieving the outcomes outlined above.

What are the benefits of a whole school approach?

A whole school scope and sequence for the teaching of thinking skills will assist in overcoming some of the less desirable practices to be observed in some schools e.g.

- the *'feast or famine syndrome'* that occurs when in one year, a class group have many opportunities to actively engage their thinking but are starved of similar opportunities the next.

- the *'We're a six-hat school syndrome'* that occurs when a single strategy is adopted by teachers and used exclusively across the school. Whilst teaching one strategy is better than teaching none, a range of strategies needs to be introduced if students are to be adequately skilled in all aspects of organising, recording and reflecting upon their thinking.

- similar to the last scenario is the the *'flavour of the month syndrome'* where, for a short period of time everyone is designing teaching and learning activities around similar frameworks or models until something 'better' comes along.

What will this mean for teachers?

Developing a thinking culture within a school will require that all teachers are familiar with a diverse range of thinking strategies so that they may use the tools of thinking:

- when planning learning activities for students, both within and across curriculum areas
- as an integral part of their classroom teaching practice
- while evaluating student learning outcomes.

It will also require teachers to employ strategies in the classroom that will include

- appropriate modelling

- explicitly teaching the tools and strategies and explaining the significance of each tool in the thinking process

- providing many opportunities for students to interact with:
  - the newly-introduced tools and strategies
  - each other
  - the teacher

as they become familiar with the tools, as they practise applying their new knowledge and then as they become confident users of the strategies in many diverse situations

- giving feedback in a variety of forms that encourages the learner to engage in both
  - risk-taking
  - reflective and metacognitive thinking.

What will students learn?

As students progress through the modules, they are exposed to a range of thinking strategies that will develop their skills in many different types of thinking which includes:-
- analytical thinking
  - critical thinking
  - creative thinking
  - metacognitive thinking
- responding to a wide range of different question types
- framing their own questions using question-generating tools
- using graphic organisers to record thinking and to present the products of their thinking
- making decisions and solving problems

What aspect of thinking is covered by each of the modules?

The scope of the modules provides the opportunity for students to receive explicit instruction in seven distinct aspects of thinking.

Choosing to introduce all modules will mean students will have covered the following concepts before they leave primary school:
- de Bono's Six Thinking
- Extended Brainstorming
- Questioning Techniques
- Tony Ryan's Thinker's Keys
- Graphic Organisers
- Bloom's Taxonomy
- Decision Making/Problem Solving

How are the modules structured?

All modules share a similar format. The content to be covered over a school year has been broken down into manageable learning tasks that could be reasonably achieved within one school term. Each module indicates the:
- suggested skills to be introduced each term
- anticipated student learning outcomes
- a brief explanation of the strategy to be taught
- some examples of learning activities which use the strategy
- proformas, student worksheets and opinionaires to assist teachers in assessing and recording student progress, achievement and attitudes
- other resources to support the introduction of the module

How should the modules be sequenced

Framing these models and strategies into a sequence for explicit teaching at specific year levels ensures that all students become familiar with all approaches to thinking in a systematic fashion - not just those most favoured by particular teachers.

In developing a whole school approach, teaching staff will decide when it is most appropriate to introduce each module.

However, extensive trialling in South Australian schools found that the order in which the modules have been presented in this book provides a logical and workable sequence that would suit most primary school settings.

Modules which introduce tools we wish students to revisit many times throughout their schooling should appear early within an agreed sequence. Explicit teaching of the more complex thinking skills should be delayed until the later years.

> The sequencing of thinking skills for classroom instruction does not preclude teachers from using tools or strategies outside of their particular year level.
>
> They will, however, follow the agreed scope and sequence for their school when focusing on the teaching of thinking skills.

Thinking Skills For Explicit Teaching Module 1
- Six Hat Thinking -

Introduction

It is suggested that teachers adopt a term-by-term approach to the teaching of the **Six Hat Thinking**, strategy.

The table on the next page provides a guide for teachers as they plan appropriate learning activities. Term content and expected student outcomes for the main elements of **Six Hat Thinking** are also given.

While teachers may choose to vary the timing of instruction of different elements to suit their planning needs, it is expected that all of the identified learning outcomes will be achieved by the time the student completes the current year of schooling.

After the table outlining the content of each module, information which will assist teachers in planning suitable classroom activities is provided. A brief description of the key strategies and examples of possible learning activities is provided.

The teaching of the module is further supported by the inclusion of proformas, student work-sheets and opinionaires that will assist in the recording of student learning outcomes, assessing levels of understanding and determining student attitudes towards the skill that has been taught. These may be photocopied for classroom use.

Other useful resources that will support the teaching of this strategy appear at the end of the module.

Module 1

- Six Hat Thinking -

Term	Strategy	Student Learning Outcomes
1	**Six Thinking Hats** (One hat at a time)	**Students can:** • explain the thinking for each hat • practise orally the appropriate thinking for each hat • give examples of yellow hat ideas, green hat ideas, etc.
2	**Hat Sequence (Evaluation)**	**Students can:** • explain the evaluation sequence • employ yellow hat and black hat thinking
3	**Hat Sequence (Caution)**	**Students can:** • explain the caution sequence • effectively employ white hat and black hat thinking
4	**Hat Sequence (Design)**	**Students can:** • explain the design sequence • effectively employ blue hat, green hat and red hat thinking

Note:
Teachers may choose to go beyond the designated sequences to include some of the alternatives outlined in this section. It is expected however that all children will be experienced in the application of the evaluation, caution and design sequences.

- Six Hat Thinking -
One Hat At A Time

Just as teachers use the metaphor *"Put on your thinking caps"* to engage student's thinking, the Six Hat Thinking strategy uses the metaphor of different coloured hats to engage students in different types of thinking.

Using the hats demonstrates to students that thinking is a skill to be learned and improved upon with practice. Six Hat Thinking provides a framework for focussed, constructive and productive thought. It acknowledges that feelings and emotions are an important part of thinking. The process is fun to teach and learn at all levels.

Each of the coloured hats stands for one kind of thinking and when a particular hat is called upon, only the type of thinking represented by that hat is allowed at that time.

In this way, students may look at an idea or issue from six very different viewpoints before deciding upon the value of an idea or upon a course of action to be taken.

The six different thinking hats developed by Edward de Bono include

RED HAT :	feelings.	Students describe how they feel about something.
YELLOW HAT :	strengths.	Students consider what is good about something.
BLACK HAT : *Purple*	weaknesses.	Students identify potential problems or difficulties.
GREEN HAT :	new ideas.	What is possible? What can this lead to?
WHITE HAT:	information.	Students access the truth about something.
BLUE HAT :	thinking.	Students consider what thinking is needed to understand or to move forward.

Activities to introduce the hats one at a time include:

AH size.

- making coloured hats,
- brainstorming words associated with each coloured hat (e.g. green hat - green grass, new growth, fresh ideas)
- making posters or mobiles to reinforce the role of each hat
- activities presented in *Six Thinking Hats for Schools* (de Bono, E. 1992 Hawker Brownlow Education).

- Six Hat Thinking -
Evaluation Sequence

Using the evaluation sequence

Using the evaluation sequence will encourage students to defer judgement until both the positive aspects and negative aspects of an idea have been considered.

It is preferential to undertake yellow hat thinking before black hat thinking.

It can sometimes be easy to overlook worthwhile ideas after a lengthy black hat thinking session. It may be useful to follow up the evaluation sequence with some green hat or red hat thinking.

Practice examples

In order to encourage transfer, teachers are encouraged to integrate the application of the thinking sequence into planned teaching and learning activities or into the course of everyday happenings where using this sequence would be appropriate.

Use the evaluation sequence to consider the positive and negative aspects of:
- spending all of your pocket money each week rather than saving some
- helping an animal that has just been hit by a passing car
- not doing your homework one night
- staying up late on a week night
- swapping toys with friends

Reprinted with permission from E. de Bono *Six Thinking Hats* Hawker Brownlow Education

- Six Hat Thinking -
Caution Sequence

White Hat

Black Hat

Using the caution sequence

Using the caution sequence will encourage students to look critically at a situation to identify potential dangers or problems.

It is preferential to consider the facts of the matter first using white hat thinking, then use the black hat to discover potential difficulties.

It may be useful to follow up the caution sequence with some blue hat or red hat thinking.

Practice examples

In order to encourage transfer, teachers are encouraged to integrate the application of the thinking sequence into planned teaching and learning activities or into the course of everyday happenings where using this sequence would be appropriate.

Use the caution sequence to consider the consequences of:
- not letting someone know where you are going
- playing in the garage without permission
- throwing most of your lunch in the bin every day
- playing a trick on a friend
- biting your fingernails

Reprinted with permission from E. de Bono *Six Thinking Hats* Hawker Brownlow Education

- Six Hat Thinking -
Design Sequence

Using the design sequence

Using the design sequence will encourage students to create new ideas, new products or improvements on existing designs. This sequence has clear links to the design, make and appraise concept often presented as part of technology lessons.

Practice examples

In order to encourage transfer, teachers are encouraged to integrate the application of the thinking sequence into planned teaching and learning activities or into the course of everyday happenings where using this sequence would be appropriate.

Use the design sequence to create:
- a better toothbrush
- an easy way to keep fit
- a quicker way to learn
- alternatives to homework
- a new way of communicating with your pet

Reprinted with permission from E. de Bono *Six Thinking Hats* Hawker Brownlow Education

- Other Six Hat Sequences -

Six Thinking Hats
Simple Sequences

Improvement

1. What are the weaknesses?

2. How can we overcome them?

First Ideas

1. What is the thinking task?

2. What do we know about the situation?

3. What ideas can we think of?

Explanation

1. What do we know about the situation?

2. What are the possible explanations?

Quick Assessment

1. What are the good points?

2. Can we summarise the good points?

Direct Action

1. How do we feel about this?

2. What are the difficulties and dangers?

Evaluation

1. What are the good points?

2. What are the difficulties and dangers?

Emotions

1. How do we feel?

2. What to we know about the situation?

3. What are the alternatives?

4. What is the conclusion?

Reprinted with permission from E. de Bono *Six Thinking Hats* Hawker Brownlow Education

– Other Six Hat Sequences –

Six Thinking Hats
Simple Sequences

Possibilities

1. What are the possibilities? 2. Can we summarise the possibilities?

Caution

1. What do we know about the situation? 2. What are the dangers?

Usable Alternatives

1. What are the possibilities? 2. Why will they work? 3. What are the weak points?

Opportunity

1. What do we know about the situation? 2. What are the good points?

Choices

1. What are the good points? 2. What are the difficulties and dangers? 2. Now how do we feel about it?

Design

1. What is the design task? 2. What are the possible designs? 3. How do we feel about each possible design?

Final Assessment

1. What are the difficulties and dangers? 2. Now how do we feel about it?

Reprinted with permission from E. de Bono *Six Thinking Hats* Hawker Brownlow Education

Assessing and Recording Student Learning Outcomes
Module 1
- Six Hat Thinking -

Assessment of Student Outcomes

In order to assess the effectiveness of the explicit teaching of the skills of thinking, teachers will need to revisit the anticipated learning outcomes described at the beginning of this module. They may then choose to use some or all of the following to assess the progress of individual students

- classroom observations
- anecdotal notes
- more formal (task- specific) achievement records
- evaluation of student products
- assessments of student attitudes

In order to guide teachers in designing suitable assessment activities, the following pages provide a range of proformas, worksheets and questionnaires that will assist in both the assessment and recording of student learning outcomes. The examples of student worksheets in this module have been designed to assess understanding of junior primary school students.

> **Note:**
> The examples that follow are designed to assess and record the student's understanding of the *thinking skill* that has just been taught, regardless of the curriculum content.
>
> Teachers will need to employ other methods suggested above when *reporting* the application of the skills to specific curriculum content, themes or topics taught.

Class Record Sheet
- Six Hat Thinking -

Note:
Revisit the student learning outcomes shown at the beginning of this module. Indicate level of student comprehension below. Show whether the student has
- been exposed to the content (EX)
- demonstrated mastery (M)

Add suitable general comments as required.

Name of Student	Six Hats- (1 at a time)	Evaluation Sequence	Caution Sequence	Design Sequence	Comment

Student Worksheet 1
- Six Hat Thinking -

Six children were talking about ice-creams.
Colour the hat to show what sort of Six Hat Thinking each person used.

I love ice-cream!

The problem with ice-cream is that it melts too quickly.

Ice-cream is made from milk.

Ice-cream makes you feel cool on hot days.

I wonder how we could measure the size of an ice-cream?

Let's invent an ice-cream that will not drip or melt!

My name is . . . .

Student Worksheet 2
- Six Hat Thinking -

Can you find the right hats to use?
Circle the correct hats.

Alisha wanted to use two different hats to think about all the facts that she knew about the beach and all the problems she might have if she went by herself.	**Red**
	Yellow
	Black
Which hat would help her discover facts about the beach?	**Green**
	White
Which hat would help her discover the possible problems?	**Blue**
Josh was thinking about spending some of his money on a new toy. He thought about all the good things about having a new toy. What hat was he wearing then?	**Red**
	Yellow
	Black
Next he thought about all the problems about buying a new toy.	**Green**
	White
What hat was he wearing then?	**Blue**

Which three hats would help you to think up a design for a new type of pencil case?	**Red Yellow Green** **or** **Black Green White** **or** **Blue Green Red** **or** **Blue White Green**
Choose the hats in the order in which you would use them.	

Student Worksheet 3
- Six Hat Thinking -

(Student Attitudes)

Draw a picture about yourself doing some Six Hat Thinking at home.

Write a sentence underneath your picture that tells what are you thinking about and why you chose that colour hat for your picture.

My favourite hat is . . . . because

Using the Six Hats can be good because . . . . .

Module Support Resources

de Bono, E. (1983)   *Cort Thinking - teachers notes 2nd Ed.*
Victoria, Hawker Brownlow Education

de Bono, E. (1986)   *Think Lanes.* Chicago: Science Research Associates
Publications

de Bono, E. (1995)   *Mind power.* USA: Allen & Unwin

de Bono, E. (1992)   *Six Thinking Hats For Schools.* Books 1-4
Victoria: Hawker Brownlow Education

Thinking Skills For Explicit Teaching
Module 2
- Extended Brainstorming -

Introduction

It is suggested that teachers adopt a term-by-term approach to the teaching of the **brainstorming strategy.**

The table on the next page provides a guide for teachers as they plan appropriate learning activities. Suggested term content, and expected student outcomes for the four main elements of extended **brainstorming** are given.

Whilst teachers may choose to vary the timing of instruction of different elements to suit their planning needs, it is expected that all identified learning outcomes will be achieved by the time the student completes the current year of schooling.

The teaching of the module is further supported by the inclusion of proformas, student worksheets and opinionaires that will assist in the recording of student learning outcomes, assessing levels of understanding and determining student attitudes towards the skill that has been taught. These may be photocopied for classroom use.

Other useful resources that will support the teaching of this strategy appear at the end of the module.

Module 2
- Extended Brainstorming -

Term	Strategy	Student Learning Outcomes
1	**Fluency** (The flood of ideas)	**Students can:** • define fluency in terms of generating ideas, possibilities or consequences • describe the elements of the brainstorming process
2	**Flexibility** (Different kinds of ideas)	**Students can:** • define developing flexibility in terms of generating different types of ideas • group brainstormed responses into categories • use tools such as 'Y' charts
3	**Originality** (Unusual or unique ideas)	**Students can:** • define originality in terms of generating unusual ideas, new approaches, novel solutions • identify original ideas from their brainstormed list
4	**Elaboration** (Expanded and developed ideas)	**Students can:** • Explore alternative means to improve upon an idea or make something more complete, effective or efficient. • expand upon ideas generated during a brainstorm.

Note:
Teachers may choose to go beyond the 4 cognitive elements of brainstorming to include the affective components of curiosity, complexity, risk-taking and imagination outlined in this module.

– Extended Brainstorming –

Fluency

Fluency ➜	Lots of Ideas Lots of Solutions Lots of Possibilities Lots of Consequences

Brainstorming for **fluency** engages students in generating many ideas around a topic. It can be undertaken as an individual activity but brainstorming is most productive when it involves small or whole class groups.

Introducing students to the acronym LACE ensures the widest possible participation during the brainstorming session.

L = Lots of ideas wanted	(so piggybacking on ideas is okay)
A = All responses recorded	(ideas are judged later)
C = Criticism is not allowed	(of people or ideas)
E = Encourage way out ideas	(it might produce a better solution in the end)

Suitable activities to develop **fluency** may involve students brainstorming around topics such as

- Names of things found underground.
- Ways to measure the passing of time?
- Things that are sweet.
- Uses for a metre of string?
- Objects with angles
- Ways to catch a Cheetah?
- What's hot?

- Extended Brainstorming -

Flexibility

Flexibility ➡️ **Different Sorts of Ideas**
Different Directions in Thinking
Adapting Thoughts
Adapting Ideas

Developing **flexibility** is an analytical task that requires students to generate many different kinds of ideas.

Whilst brainstorming for fluency is a common practice in many classrooms, the process is easily extended when students analyse responses and group them in as many ways as they can. This can lead to the discovery of other categories and other ideas to add within existing categories of responses. In this way **flexibility** becomes a valuable extension to the original brainstorm.

As with brainstorming for fluency, developing flexible thinking can be undertaken as an individual activity but is most productive when it involves small or whole class groups.

Suitable activities to develop **flexibility** may include

- Group words brainstormed about outer space into as many categories as you can.
  Then think of other ways to group them, new categories to use or other words to add under each category heading.

- How many different ways might you_____?

- Compare a chicken to an eagle. In how many ways are they the same and in how many ways are they different?

- Use the acronym **SCUMPS** (Size, Colour, Uses, Materials, Parts, Shape) to find similarities and differences between unrelated objects, e.g. a tree and a bedsock.

- Give as many different reasons as you can for .....

- Extended Brainstorming -
Originality

| Originality | ➡ | A New Idea
A Better Idea
An Unusual idea |

Originality is a creative thinking task that engages students in searching for new ideas, better ways of doing things or unique or untried solutions to problems.

It can be seen as a logical extension to the previous two processes and is easily introduced once brainstorming for fluency and brainstorming for flexibility is well understood by students.

Originality asks students to imagine the imaginable, to consider the impossible and reject everyday explanations. It would be appropriate then, to review the **LACE** procedures to ensure successful participation and the generation of more unusual responses.

From a previous brainstorm, students are encouraged to find the most original ideas (often the most off-beat) and give them serious consideration. The result is often that this first ìway-outî idea will lead to further ideas grounded more in reality. Suddenly original, workable solutions are discovered as a result.

Suitable activities to develop **originality**:

*   Imagine you are only 30 centimetres tall. How would your world be different?
*   Create a new number system.
*   Use the attributes of a television quiz show to help you design and market a new breakfast cereal. (Using the acronym SCUMPS introduced earlier may be useful).
*   Describe a new animal which would have some distinct advantages for humans that many other animals do not have.
*   Compose a ....
*   Combine attributes of a tennis ball, a television monitor and jelly crystals to invent a new team sport.

- Extended Brainstorming -

Elaboration

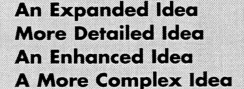

Elaboration ➡ An Expanded Idea
More Detailed Idea
An Enhanced Idea
A More Complex Idea

Engaging students in **elaboration** involves making existing ideas or objects more detailed, more interesting or useful in situations otherwise not considered.

Elaboration develops both creative thinking and critical thinking as students decide between alternatives, weigh up relative advantages and make decisions based on self-devised criteria.

It can be seen as a logical extension to the process of originality. Students build upon the creative responses generated from earlier brainstorming sessions.

Suitable activities to develop student skills in **elaboration**:

- Embellish a milk carton to make it more useful or more attractive
- Add a new character to an existing story. How does this effect the events in the story?
- Design a new logo for your school which builds upon some of the elements of the existing design but makes it more relevant for today.
- Use the **BAR** (Bigger, Add, Replace) technique described in Module 4 to design a better lawnmower.
- Substitute an ingredient in a cake mix to create a new variety.
- Modify a mobile phone so that is more user-friendly.
- Improve on the design of an existing.........
- Change the way that we .... to make it more efficient, cheaper or easier to do.

Assessing and Recording Student Learning Outcomes
- Extended Brainstorming -

In order to assess the effectiveness of the explicit teaching of the skills of thinking, teachers will need to revisit the anticipated learning outcomes described at the beginning of this module. They may then choose to use some or all of the following to assess the progress of individual students

- classroom observations
- anecdotal notes
- more formal (task-specific) achievement records
- evaluation of student products
- assessments of student attitudes

In order to guide teachers in designing suitable assessment activities, the following pages provide a range of proformas, worksheets and questionnaires that will assist in both the assessment and recording of student learning outcomes. The examples of student worksheets in this model have been designed to assess understanding of junior primary age children.

Note:
The examples that follow are designed to assess and record the student's understanding of the thinking skill that has just been taught, regardless of the curriculum content.

Teachers will need to employ other methods as suggested above when reporting the application of the skills to specific curriculum content, themes or topics taught.

Class Record Sheet
- Extended Brainstorming -

Note:
Revisit the student learning outcomes shown at the beginning of this module. Indicate level of student comprehension below. Show whether the student has
- been exposed to content (EX)
- demonstrated mastery (M)

Add suitable general comments

Name of	Fluency	Flexibility	Originality	Elaboration	Comment

Student Worksheet 1
- Extended Brainstorming -

Draw a line to match the sentence beginnings on the left side of the page with the sentence endings on the right side of the page so that the sentence is TRUE.

Fluency is all about ...

... finding some new or very different ideas that not many other people would think up

Flexibility is all about ...

... adding lots of details to our ideas to make it easier for others to understand or to make it more interesting.

Originality is all about ...

... coming up with lots of ideas.

Elaboration is all about ...

... coming up with lots of different sorts of ideas.

Cross out the sentences that are not true about BRAINSTORMING.
When we brainstorm ....

We write down every idea that we are given.
We write down only the ideas that we want to write down.

It **is not** okay to 'piggy-back' on other people's ideas.
It **is** okay to 'piggy-back' on other people's ideas.

We **should not** give 'way-out' ideas.
We **should** try to give some 'way-out' ideas.

It's okay to make fun of other people's ideas.
It is not okay to make fun of other people's ideas.

Look over your answers and when you know you have done everything that you can, write your name below.

My name is _____

Student Worksheet 2

What do YOU know about .... Brainstorming???

Think about a time when your teacher asked you to do some brainstorming. What did you do? Write on the back of this page if you run out of room.

What do YOU think about .... Brainstorming???

Is brainstorming fun? _____ Why do you think so?

Why do you think people brainstorm ideas?

Is brainstorming something you can do with your friends? ____
Why do you think so?

Do you think older people brainstorm?_____
Why?

Do you think you will brainstorm for ideas when you are older? _____
Why do you think so?

When do you think it might be a good idea to brainstorm for ideas at home?

Module Support Resources

Black, H. et. al. (1992)   *Tracks - pathways for gifted children..* Cammeray, NSW: Martin Education

Dalton, J. (1990)   *Adventures in Thinking.* South Melbourne: Thomas Nelson.

Deutsch, G. (1993)   *Creative problem solving for young people.* Victoria: Hawker Brownlow Education

Dickinson ,et.al. (1987)   *Brainstorming - activities for creative thinking.* Sunnyvale, CA: Creative Publications.

Fligor, M. (1993)   *Brainstorming - the book of topics.* Victoria: Hawker Brownlow Education.

McAuliffe, J. & Stoskin, L. (1994)   *What colour is Saturday?* Victoria: Hawker Brownlow Education.

Thomson, P. (1993)   *Brightsparks - critical and creative thinking.* Melbourne: Longman Cheshire.

Williams, F.(1970)   *Classroom ideas for encouraging thinking and feeling.* Victoria: Hawker Brownlow Education.

Thinking Skills For Explicit Teaching
Module 3
- Questioning Techniques -

Introduction

It is suggested that teachers adopt a term-by-term approach to the teaching of **questioning techniques**.

The table on the next page provides a guide for teachers as they plan appropriate learning activities. Suggested term content, and expected student outcomes are given for all types of **questioning techniques** introduced.

While teachers may choose to vary the timing of instruction of different elements to suit their planning needs, it is expected that all identified learning outcomes will be achieved by the time the student completes the current year of schooling.

The teaching of the module is further supported by the inclusion of proformas, student work-sheets and opinionaires that will assist in the recording of student learning outcomes, assessing levels of understanding and determining student attitudes towards the skill that has been taught. These may be photocopied for classroom use.

Other useful resources which will support the teaching of this strategy appear at the end of the module.

Module 3
- Questioning Techniques -

Term	Strategy	Student Learning Outcomes
1	**Open & Closed Questions**	**Students can:** • classify questions as open or closed • explain differences between open and closed questions • change a closed question into an open question • formulate their own open and closed questions
2	**Fat & Skinny Questions**	**Students can:** • classify questions as fat or skinny • explain differences between fat and skinny questions • change a skinny question into a fat question • formulate their own fat and skinny questions
3	**Student-Generated Questions**	**Students can:** • use both the matrix grid and matrix cubes to generate questions within a curriculum area • identify whether questions generated are open or closed, fat or skinny
4	**Student-Generated Questions**	**In groups, students can:** • generate questions for a curriculum topic or cross-curriculum investigation using the ICE principle

- Questioning Techniques -

Type of Question	Type of Thinking	Type of Response	Example
Closed	Convergent	**Yes/No** Single ("correct") answer or Finite number of (agreed) answers.	Is the sun a star? What type of mammal is a platypus? What are the months of the year?
Open	Divergent	Many possible responses. Not one "correct" answer.	How could the environment of the school be improved? How would the story have been different if it was in the future?
Skinny	Simple	Little elaboration required. Often closed requiring basic knowledge and comprehension	What makes an atom? What day comes 3 days after Monday?
Fat	Complex	Interpretation required. May involve critical/creative thinking (i.e. higher levels of Bloom's taxonomy)	Is it ever OK to tease someone? Why do you think this? What would you change to improve your pencil case? Explain your changes.

- Open and Closed
Fat and Skinny Questions -

Questions are sometimes classified as open, closed, fat or skinny.
When considered together, a matrix of four possible question types becomes apparent.
The relatonship between open and closed, fat and skinny questions is concerned with the nature and degree of complexity of thinking required to arrive at an answer.
The Australian animals example makes explicit the relationship between the four different question types.

This question is
Skinny.
It is simple, with little elaboration required in the reply.
It is also
Closed.
It requires convergent thinking with a finite number of agreed answers.

This question is
Skinny.
It is simple and requires little elaboration.
It is also
Open.
It requires divergent thinking generating many possible responses.

	Closed	Open
Skinny	One Australian animal that lays eggs is…	Ten Australian animals that are not mammals include…
Fat	List 5 ways that a dingo and a poodle are similar.	What would happen if all koalas in Australia disappeared? Give many possibilities.

This question is
Fat.
It is complex and requires a degree of interpretation.
It is also
Closed.
It requires a finite number of agreed answers.

This question is
Fat.
It is complex and requires a degree of interpretation.
It is also
Open.
It requires divergent thinking generating many possible responses.

Background Information for Teachers
- Student-Generated Questions -

Teachers are encouraged to have students devise a range of questions around a topic or idea. This process can be valuable:

- for specific skill development (for example group skills or communication skills when undertaken as a group task). When placed in heterogeneous ability groups, good questioners can share their skills with those who find framing questions more difficult.

- to allow for independent study and pupil involvement in their own learning. Students will find that developing their own questions is an empowering process. It will also overcome that often-asked question: "Why are we doing this?".

- in conjunction with other tools to develop thinking skills (for example Thinker's Keys).

Once students have been introduced to various types of questions, including fat and skinny questions and open and closed questions, they can be encouraged to suggest questions of their own.

Providing a focus will help in the process. The well-tried examples of asking Who..., What..., When..., Where..., Why... and How... will help students consider the topic from a range of perspectives.

We can then encourage students to ask questions such as
> How do we feel about...?
> Can we say what we like about...?
> What problems might be involved in...?
> How might the effect be if I change...?
> Can I predict what might happen if...?
> What are some other ways of...?
> How can I find out more about...?

An excellent tool is the Question Matrix (Kagan 1994; Wiederhold 1991): a 36-square grid of question starters that will assist students to develop their own questions – see Module Support Resources at the end of this section.

Background Information for Teachers
- Student-Generated Questions -

Where are some opportunities for students to be involved in developing their own questions?
Here are just a few possibilities.

LANGUAGE Responding to reading	• questions about plot, characters, events • basis of individual contract work
Oral Language	• morning news, guest speakers, class meetings

Writing	• predictive questions to plan story, set scene, characters, etc.
	    What if the story took place in... ?
	    What will the main character do next?
	    How would the story end differently if... ?

MATHEMATICS	• questions about the concept under study, e.g.
	    How and where is this type of measurement used in real life?
	    How did you arrive at that answer?
	    What will happen if you leave off a zero?

SCIENCE	• particularly relevant to generate research-based questions or topics, questions for enquiry, investigations, for example *What questions could we ask about the weather, space, medicine, magnets?*

TECHNOLOGY	• formulating a Planning and Design task, for example
	    Who might use this new play equipment? How can we improve upon our design?
	    How might we market our equipment?

SOCIETY & ENVIRONMENT	• research or review questions • planning topics, excursions, learning activities
HEALTH & PHYSICAL EDUCATION	• questions designed by children around a topic may assist teachers to plan a unit of work, for example *What questions do we need to ask in designing a better fitness program?*
ARTS	• planning a performance • research and review • designing a product or piece of art.

- Students as Questioners -

If we are serious about encouraging student engagement and student ownership of their own learning, then opportunities for students to be involved in the planning stages of learning activities can only serve to encourage such an outcome.

Student Generated Questions

Ideally we want students to generate not just any questions, but questions that are truly worthy of investigation.

Questions that build the knowledge-base of students; that seek to engage them in exploring consequences and alternatives and questions that will take understanding to a deeper level would clearly be worthy of investigation.

Here, the **ICE PRINCIPLE** may be a useful guide for students as they work together to formulate possible questions for inclusion in individual assignments or group research.

Ice Principle

Formulate questions that are:

INVESTIGATIVE – that generate information about NOW and THEN

CONSEQUENTIAL – that explore possible IMPACTS and OUTCOMES

ENRICHING – that require CRITICAL, CREATIVE or CARING thinking responses.

The bottom line is that we, as teachers, wish to see students creating not just many questions, but many *different kinds* of questions: some that generate new ways of looking at things; some that require a good deal of elaboration and some that require students to continually shift from convergent to divergent thought processes.

ICE PRINCIPLE

Examples of Question Starters

INVESTIGATIVE: Generating information about NOW and THEN

Can we list things...?	Can we find some examples of...?
Who's responsible for...?	What happened when...?
What events assisted...?	Why did/didn't...?
When does...?	Where could/couldn't one find...?
What is/was meant by...?	What happened before/after...?
How many...?	Who suggested that...?
Who was it that...?	Can you name...?
What is clearly true...?	What is clearly false...?

Hint:
Questions containing "are" and "is" will often assist in generating investigative questions. These questions focus on facts and what is already known.

CONSEQUENTIAL: Exploring possible IMPACTS and OUTCOMES
Hint:

What are some effects of...?	How is this similar to...?
In what ways is this different from...?	What factors contributed to...?
Can this be compared with...?	Can this be simplified by...?
Short-term consequences might be...	Long-term consequences might be...
Who else might have a different view?	Others might think...
A different perspective might be...	What else needs to be considered?
Can you group by characteristics such as...?	What questions would you ask of...?

A focus on questions that analyse what could or couldn't happen, or compare and contrast both like and unlike scenarios will assist in generating consequential questions. These questions focus on what might happen as a result of a given circumstance.

ENRICHING: Require a CRITICAL / CREATIVE / CARING thinking responses.

Is there a better solution to...?	Judge the value of...
What is your opinion of...?	How would you have handled...?
Can you defend your position about...?	How many ways can you...?
What changes to... would you recommend?	Can you see a possible solution to...?
How effective are...?	What plan might we adopt to...?
What would happen if...?	What emotions are stirred when...?
Can you develop a proposal which would...?	How might others feel should... happen?

Hint:
'What do you think' and 'Why' will evoke a critical thinking response.
'What if' questions focus on creative alternatives.
'How might you/others feel' will engender an affective (caring) response.

Assessing and Recording Student Learning Outcomes Module 3 - Questioning Techniques -

Assessment of Student Outcomes

To assess the effectiveness of explicitly teaching thinking skills, teachers will need to revisit the anticipated learning outcomes described at the beginning of this module. They may then choose to use some or all of the following means to assess the progress of individual students.

- Classroom observations
- Anecdotal notes
- More formal (task-specific) achievement records
- Evaluation of student products
- Assessments of student attitudes

The following pages provide a range of proformas, worksheets and questionnaires that will assist in both the assessment and recording of student learning outcomes. The examples of student worksheets in this model have been designed to assess understanding of junior-primary age children.

Note:
The examples that follow are designed to assess and record the student's understanding of the thinking skill that has just been taught, regardless of the curriculum content.

Teachers will need to employ other methods as suggested above when reporting the application of the skills to specific curriculum content, themes or topics.

Class Record Sheet
- Questioning Techniques -

Notes:
Revisit the student learning outcomes shown at the beginning of this module. Indicate level of student comprehension below. Show whether the student has
• been exposed to content (EX)
• demonstrated mastery (M).
Add suitable general comments.

Name of Student	Fat/Skinny Questions	Open/Closed Questions	Student-Generated Questions	Comment

Student Worksheet 1

Here are some activities about questions for you to try.

Which of these questions are OPEN and which are CLOSED?
Circle the correct answer.

Is the sun a plane?	Open/Closed
How could we improve the school day?	Open/Closed
How would a story be different if you were the main character?	Open/Closed
How many different uses can you find for a toothpick?	Open/Closed
What sort of animal is a whale?	Open/Closed
What are the names of the days of the week?	Open/Closed

Why is "How many legs are there on a dog?" a skinny question?

Why is "Why are there so many different types of dogs?" a fat question?

Pretend that a visitor comes into your classroom one day when you are doing a question-generating activity. Explain what you are doing and how you are using the ICE principle.

My name is _____

Student Worksheet 2

What do YOU think about ... Questions ????

Which questions are more interesting – **open or closed?** Why do you think so?

Can you think of a time when it might be better to ask a **Skinny Question** rather than a **Fat Question?** Explain your answer.

Pretend you have been asked to make up questions of your own for a project on animals. Would you find using **ICE questioning** helpful? Explain your answer.

Think of a time when you might use the **ICE questions** when you are older and not at school. Explain how you might use it and why.

My name is _____

Module Support Resources

Dalton, J. (1990)

Adventures in thinking. Melbourne: Thomas Nelson.

Fogarty, R. & Bellanca, J. (1989)

Patterns for thinking - patterns for transfer,
Victoria: Hawker Brownlow Education.

Kagan, S. (1994)

Cooperative Learning. California: Kagan Cooperative
Learning.

Langrehr, J. (1993)

Better questions, better thinking, books 1 & 2.
Sydney: Longman Cheshire.

Langrehr, J. (1994)

Become a better thinker. Victoria: Wrightbooks.

Langrehr, J. (1995)

Thinking chips for thinking students.
Victoria: Hawker Brownlow Education.

Perry, C. (1994)

Questioning makes the difference.
Victoria: Hawker Brownlow Education.

Wiederhold, C. (1991)

Co-operative learning and critical thinking.
The question matrix. San Juan Capistrano,
CA: Resources for Teachers.

Thinking Skills For Explicit Teaching Module 4 Thinker's Keys

Introduction

It is suggested that teachers adopt a term-by-term approach to the teaching of the **Thinker's Keys**.

The table on the next page provides a guide for teachers as they plan appropriate learning activities. Suggested term content and expected student outcomes are given for eight different **Thinker's Keys**.

While teachers may choose to vary the timing of instruction of different elements to suit their planning needs, it is expected that all identified learning outcomes will be achieved by the time the student completes the current year of schooling.

The teaching of the module is further supported by the inclusion of proformas, student work-sheets and opinionaires that will assist in the recording of student learning outcomes, assessing levels of understanding and determining student attitudes towards the skill that has been taught. These may be photocopied for classroom use.

Some useful resources which will support the teaching of this strategy appear at the end of the module.

Module 4
- Thinker's Keys -

Term	Strategy	Student Learning Outcomes
1	**Alphabet KEY**	**Students can:** • compile a list of words from A-Z of objects, features of an object or a topic under consideration
	Disadvantages KEY	• list disadvantages of an object or idea • offer improvements to correct or eliminate disadvantages
2	**Reverse Key**	**Students can:** • use knowledge to consider questions that contain words such as cannot, never and not in developing flexible thinking (eg 10 things you could not clean)
	What if... KEY	• generate a range of both positive and negative responses to a scenario that begins with 'What if...'
3	**BAR KEY**	**Students can:** • demonstrate the use of the BAR technique
	Construction KEY	• demonstrate practical creative thinking through the construction of structures using limited quantities of readily available materials
4	**Picture KEY**	**Students can:** • demonstrate flexible and creative thinking by linking a simple (unrelated) line drawing to the current topic or idea
	Question Key	• devise a set number of questions given the answer as a starting point (e.g. the answer is MIDNIGHT. List 5 questions).

Note:
Teachers may choose to go beyond using the designated keys to include some of the other keys suggested in Tony Ryan's (1990) *Thinker's Keys for Kids*. It is expected that all children will be experienced in the use of the eight keys described above.

- Thinker's Keys -

Alphabet Key

Find related topic words for every letter of the alphabet for this word -

....

→ A restricted form of brainstorming that is an excellent tool for establishing current knowledge levels.

A tool that encourages both critical and creative thinking as students identify faults and then suggest improvements to everyday objects. ←

Disadvantages Key

List disadvantages of ....

Now correct, eliminate, modify parts to improve upon the original design.

Reverse Key

List the things that you could never

....

....?

→ Students engage in flexible thinking as they identify things that they could never see, do, touch, hear, etc.

This analytical task draws upon existing knowledge of students and can generate many innovative ideas. (Can be used in conjunction with the consequence wheel - see Module 5) ←

What if... Key

What would be the consequences of

....

....

- Thinker's Keys -

Bar Key

Make something bigger, add to it, replace something.

Start with ....

Using the acronym **Bar**, students redesign everyday items as they make one part **Bigger**, **Add** something and **Replace** another part to create a novel product.

A problem solving task that requires the creative use of limited quantities of everyday materials.

Construction Key

Build a structure to hold a model car at least a metre from the floor using only one newspaper, a metre of masking tape and 10 straws.

Picture Key

How does this picture link to the topic?

Find many solutions.

Students are forced to forge links between given content and an unrelated picture. An activity that encourages visualisation and creative thinking.

Flexible thinking is required as students come at a problem from the opposite direction. Excellent introductory activity to establish current knowledge of a subject.

Question Key

The answer is Bananas.

What are some possible questions?

- Simple Learning Activity -
- The Circus -

Alphabet Key

Find related topic works for every letter of the alphabet for this word -
CIRCUS.

Disadvantages Key

List disadvantages of a lion's cage.
Now correct, eliminate, modify parts to improve upon the original design.

Reverse Key

List the things that you would never see at the circus.

What if... Key

What if.................................
there were no circuses?

Bar Key

Make something bigger, add to it, replace something.
Start with .... a circus tent.

Construction Key

Build a model of a high-wire trapeze using a metre of string, one newspaper, a metre of masking tape and 20 straws.

Picture Key

How does this picture link to the circus? Find many solutions.

Question Key

The answer is **Ringmaster**.
What are some possible questions?

Assessing And Recording Student Learning Outcomes
Module 4
Thinker's Keys

Assessment Of Student Outcomes

In order to assess the effectiveness of the explicit teaching of the skills of thinking, teachers will need to revisit the anticipated learning outcomes described at the beginning of this module. They may then choose to use some or all of the following means to assess the progress of individual students

- classroom observations
- anecdotal notes
- more formal (task-specific) achievement records
- evaluation of student products
- assessments of student attitudes

In order to assist teachers in designing suitable assessment activities, the following pages provide a range of proformas, worksheets and questionnaires that will assist in both the assessment and recording of student learning outcomes. The examples of student worksheets in this module have been designed to assess understanding of lower primary age children.

> **Note:**
> The examples that follow are designed to assess and record the student's understanding of the thinking skill that has just been taught, regardless of the curriculum content.
>
> Teachers will need to employ other methods as suggested above when reporting the application of the skills to specific curriculum content, themes or topics taught.

Class Record Sheet
Thinker's Keys

Note:
Revisit the student learning outcomes shown at the beginning of this module. Indicate level of student comprehension below. Show whether the student has
- been exposed to content (EX)
- demonstrated mastery (M)

Add suitable general comments.

Name of Student	Alphabet	Disad vantage	Reverse	What if..	Comment

Class Record Sheet
Thinker's Keys

Note:
Revisit the student learning outcomes shown at the beginning of this module. Indicate level of student comprehension below. Show whether the student has
- been exposed to content (EX)
- demonstrated mastery (M)

Add suitable general comments.

Name of Student	Bar	Const-ruction	Picture	Question	Comment

Student Worksheet 1

Below are 8 activities that have been designed using 8 different thinker's keys. Draw a line to match each activity with the correct key?

Alphabet Key	What if all cars were to be banned
Disadvantage Key	Make a bridge using newspaper, string and sticky tape.
Reverse Key	List some problems with using a computer. How could some of the problems be eliminated so computers may be easier to use?
What if... Key	The answer is 12. Write five questions.
BAR Key	List 5 things that you could never touch.
Construction Key	Design a better skateboard by making one part bigger, add something and replace something.
Picture Key	Write a list of words to do with sports - one word for each letter of the alphabet.
Question Key	What might this picture have to do with tigers?

Zerg from the planet Zeron watched you as you were doing a Thinker's Key activity. Explain to him what you were doing and how the Thinker's Keys helped you with your thinking at the time.

Student Worksheet 2

What do YOU think about ... The Thinker's Keys????

Imagine that you are asked to write **4** different thinker's keys activities about animals for the class.

What keys would you choose? Say why you chose each key.

1.

2.

3.

4.

Would you enjoy creating your own activities using the keys? Why?

Which key do you find:

- the most fun to use_____

- challenges your thinking the most _____

- easiest to use _____

- gives you lots of great ideas _____

Think of a time that you might need to use thinker's keys to help you to solve a problem when you are older. Tell about your problem, the keys you might use and why you selected them.

Module Support Resources

Ryan T. (1990)   *Thinker's Keys* for Kids. Woodridge,
Qld: Logan West School Support Centre

Ryan T. (1990)   *Kid's Cards 1* - Communication, Christmas,   Outer Space,
Australiana, The Future, Environment,
Woodridge, Qld: Logan West School Support Centre

Ryan T. (1990)   *Kid's Cards 2* - Advertising, Camping, Transport, Animals, Road
Safety, Computers, Woodridge,
Qld: Logan West School Support Centre

Ryan T. (1990)   *Kid's Cards 3* - Seasons, Food, Excursions, School, Rock,
Music, Books.
Woodridge, Qld: Logan West School Support Centre

Ryan T. (1990)   *Kid's Cards 4* - Bushrangers, Tourism, Politics, Melbourne
Cup, Exhibitions, Leisure, Woodridge, Qld: Logan West School
Support Centre

Ryan T. (1994)   *Brainstorms*, Fingal, NSW: Headfirst Publishing

Ryan T. (1996)   *Mindlinks*, Fingal, NSW: Headfirst Publishing

Ryan T (1996)   *Wrapped in Living!*. Finigal, NSW: Headfirst Publishing

Thinking Skills For Explicit Teaching Module 5
- Graphic Organisers -

Introduction

It is suggested that teachers adopt a term-by-term approach to the teaching of the **graphic (visual) organisers**.

The table on the next page provides a guide for teachers as they plan appropriate learning activities. Suggested term content and expected student outcomes are given for eight **graphic organisers** to be introduced.

Whilst teachers may choose to vary the timing of instruction of different elements to suit their planning needs, it is expected that all identified learning outcomes will be achieved by the time the student completes the current year of schooling.

The teaching of the module is further supported by the inclusion of proformas, student worksheets and opinionaires that will assist in the recording of student learning outcomes, assessing levels of understanding and determining student attitudes towards the skill that has been taught. These may be photocopied for classroom use.

Some useful resources which will support the teaching of this strategy appear at the end of the module.

Module 5
Graphic Organisers

Term	Strategy	Student Learning Outcomes
1	**Simple Webb** **Concept Map**	**Students can:** • analyse attributes of an object, situation or idea and display as a simple web diagram • demonstrate the ability to extend the simple web.
2.	**Venn Diagram** **Consequence Wheel**	**Students Can:** • explain and demonstrate the Venn diagram • explain and demonstrate the Consequence Wheel
3	**Fishbone** **Flow Chart**	**Students Can:** • explain and demonstrate the Fishbone as a diagrammatic tool • explain and demonstrate the flow chart as a visual representation • can use a flow chart to demonstrate the recording of a simple sequence
4	**Matrix** **Mindmap**	**Students Can:** • display the ability to categorise and analyse information • demonstrates the ability to use words, drawings and colour to map out relationships

Note:
Teachers may choose to vary the time at which particular skills are introduced through the year or may choose to introduce additional graphic organisers as appropriate.
Organising Thinking Book 2 by Parks S. & Black (1993) and *Co-operative Think Tank I & II* R. Fogarty, J. Bellanca serve as excellent resources for teachers.

Using Graphic Organisers For Teaching and Learning

Students Use Graphic Organisers To...		*Teachers Use Graphic Organisers To...*	
Manage	• their own thinking • their own learning	**Model**	• the tools for organising and recording thinking • graphic organisers as a means of simplifying complex material for more abstract examination/ analysis/evaluation
Organise	• their ideas • their reports • their presentations		
Record	• products of their thinking • products of their research	**Provide**	• visual links between thinking processes and subject content • learning opportunities for visual learners and learners with limited language skills
Depict	• relationships between people • relationships between events • relationships between ideas and concepts • sequences of events	**Prepare**	• program layouts • wall displays • timetables • presentations
Improve	• retention of information • recall of information • quality of written or oral presentations	**Demonstrate**	• complex relationships and inter-relationships
		Improve	• the effectiveness of their own teaching

- Graphic Organisers -

Simple Webbing

Simple webbing engages students in analytical thinking as they use a diagram to record the components of a central topic, concept or situation. It is an excellent way to depict the products of an individual, group or whole class brainstorm around a topic.

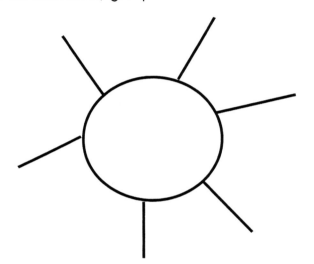

- The central concept is written in the centre of the circle.

- Students record the elements associated with the central concept on spokes that radiate from the centre.

- Extra spokes may be added as required.

Concept Maps

Concept maps are more complex variations on the simple webbing technique described above. Three different concepts maps are introduced below. They are the spider map, the cycle map and the concept layer map.

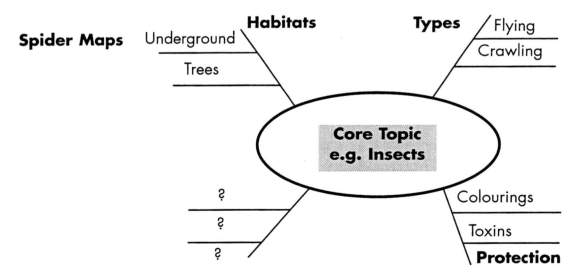

Spider maps identify major aspects of the core topic and provide a further simplified breakdown of each component.

More lines may be added to include all sub-topics and additional components.

- Graphic Organisers -

Cycle Maps

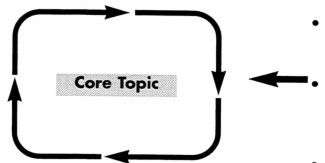

- The central concept is written in the centre of the circle.

- Students record the stages that are of a cyclic nature or record the usual direction or sequence of events.

- Useful for showing such things as life cycles, natural phenomena (e.g. precipitation formation) and economic chain of events

Concept Layer Maps

A concept layer map is a more complex variation on the simple webbing technique described before.

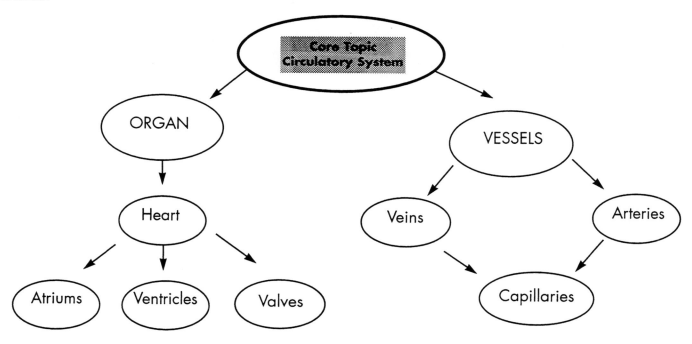

Concept layer maps identify major aspects of the core concept and then related sub-concepts in ever decreasing size or degree of complexity.

More connections may be added to include all sub-topics and additional components.

- Graphic Organisers -

Venn Diagrams

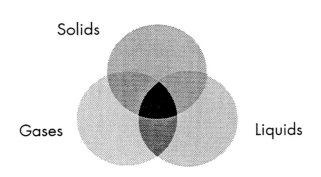

Solids

Gases   Liquids

- an excellent tool to compare and contrast two or more people, places, events, stories or objects

- a tool to depict the products of analytical thinking
- the example at left requires students to categorise elements and compounds found in nature (e.g. water, air, oxygen, gold, etc.).

Consequence Wheel

It often leads to innovative ideas so the consequence wheel can be as much a tool for creative thinking as it is a tool for analytical thinking as well.

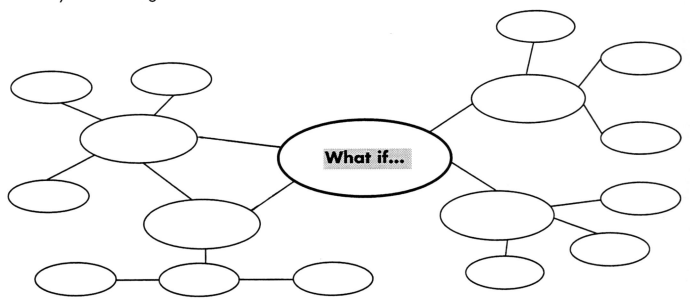

What if...

Given a **'What if...'** scenario, students record the possible consequences on the shapes that join the centre ellipse. Subsequent consequences are brainstormed and recorded on the smallest ellipses around the outside.

The consequence wheel may be expanded as more consequences are discovered.

This graphic organiser is an excellent tool to use in conjunction with the **'What if...'** key described in Module 4.

- Graphic Organisers -

Fishbone Diagram

Using a fishbone engages students in analytical thinking as they use a diagram to record the possible causes of a given effect.

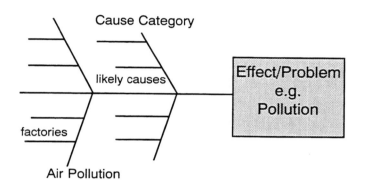

- The effect is noted in the fish 'head'- e.g. pollution.
- Categories of possible causes are recorded on the oblique *'bones'* of the fish - e.g. air pollution, water pollution ,etc.
- Possible cause elements are recorded on the finer lateral *'bones'*.

Flow Charts

Flow charts are diagrammatic representation of sequences, actions or steps taken in arriving at solutions or in making decisions.

Flow charts can be used to show sequences, such as
- routines to follow steps in a construction of a model, etc.
- *'How to'* instructions eg load a computer program, make a cake, etc.

Flow charts are also useful to indicate specific processes such as how to write in a particular style (e.g. a resume, a recipe, etc.)

They are also used to show
- how decisions can be reached
- the consequences of taking certain paths
- the steps to consider during a planning process.

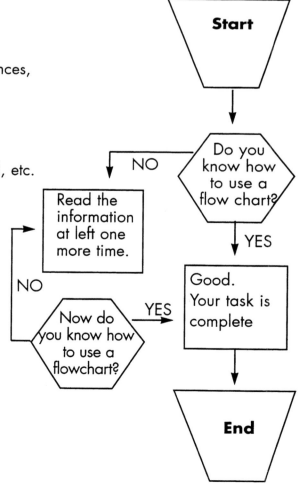

- Graphic Organisers -

The Matrix

The matrix cross-references information. Timetables, costing details and statistical reports are common examples. They allow for easy access to specific information and are useful in drawing comparisons.

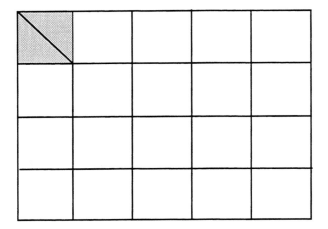

- Decide on the number of headings for columns and rows
- Label each one
- Record the appropriate information in each box
- Use it to
  - record data collected
  - compare figures, events, patterns, functions, point out similarities or differences

Mind mapping

Mind mapping is a logical extension to the concept mapping techniques described earlier. Based on research which demonstrates that the brain recalls pictures and patterns more easily than words or numbers alone, it is a strategy which involves the drawing of any number of branching lines from a common centre point.
Colour, sketches, and dimension are added to enhance the mindmap.

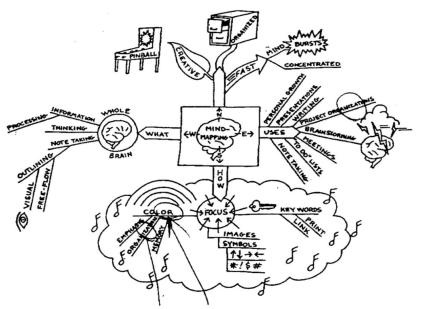

Assessing and Recording Student Learning Outcomes
Module 5
- Graphic Organisers -

In order to assess the effectiveness of the explicit teaching of the skills of thinking, teachers will need to revisit the anticipated learning outcomes described at the beginning of this module. They may then choose to use some or all of the following means to assess the progress of individual students

- classroom observations
- anecdotal notes
- more formal (task-specific) achievement records
- evaluation of student products
- assessments of student attitudes

In order to assist teachers in designing suitable assessment activities, the following pages provide a range of proformas, worksheets and questionnaires that will assist in both the assessment and recording of student learning outcomes. The examples of student worksheets in this module have been designed to assess understanding of lower primary age children.

Note:

The examples that follow are designed to assess and record the student's understanding of the thinking skill that has just been taught, regardless of the curriculum content.

Teachers will need to employ other methods as suggested above when reporting the application of the skills to specific curriculum content, themes or topics taught.

Class Record Sheet
Graphic Organisers

Note:
Revisit the student learning outcomes shown at the beginning of this module. Indicate level of student comprehension below. Indicate whether the student has:
- been exposed to the context (EX)
- demonstrated mastery (M)

Add comments as required

Name of Student	Webbing	Concept Map	Venn Diagram	Consequence Wheel	Comment

Class Record Sheet
Graphic Organisers

Note:

Revisit the student learning outcomes shown at the beginning of this module. Indicate level of student comprehension below. Indicate whether the student has:

- been exposed to the context (EX)
- demonstrated mastery (M)

Add comments as required

Name of Student	Fishbone	Flow Charts	The Matrix	Mind Map	Comment

Student Worksheet 1

Draw a line to match the diagrams with the correct names for each one.

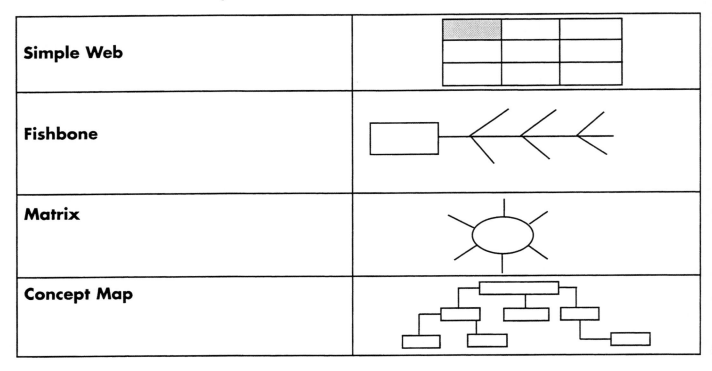

Simple Web	
Fishbone	
Matrix	
Concept Map	

Draw a line to match the names of the diagrams with the way that we might use them.

To show thinking using words, colours, pictures and lines we could use a...	Venn Diagram
To show the steps or stages that we pass through as we reach a solution or arrive at a suitable end point we could use a...	Flow Chart
To show similarities and differences between 2 or more things we could use a...	Consequence Wheel
A useful tool for recording our thinking when we ask "What if..." questions could be a...	Mind Map

Student Worksheet 2

What do YOU think about... Graphic Organisers?

Why do you think it might sometimes be better to show your thinking in drawings and diagrams rather than have to write about it in detail?

Tell about a graphic organiser that you enjoyed using this year. Why did you like to use it?

Can you list at least three graphic organisers that you think you might use when you are older and have left school? Explain how or when you might use them.

May be reproduced for classroom use

Module Support Resources

Bellanca, J. &
Fogarty, R. (1989)

Patterns for thinking, patterns for transfer.
Victoria: Hawker Brownlow Education

Bellanca, J. &
Fogarty, R. (1991)

Blueprints for thinking in the cooperative classroom.
Victoria: Hawker Brownlow Education.

Buzan, T. (1995)

The mind map book. London: BBC Books

Langrehr, J.(1994)

Become a better thinker. North Brighton Victoria: Wrightbooks

Langrehr, J.(1996)

Thinking chips for thinking students. Victoria:
Hawker Brownlow Education.

Margulies, N. (1992)

Mapping inner space. Victoria: Hawker Brownlow Education

Parks, S. &
Black, H. (1990)

Organising thinking - graphic organisers. Books I & II.
Victoria: Hawker Brownlow Education.

Thinking Skills For Explicit Teaching
Module 6
Bloom's Taxonomy

Introduction

It is suggested that teachers adopt a term-by-term approach to the teaching of the newly revised **Bloom's Taxonomy**, culminating in a student-designed project around a negotiated topic.

The table on the next page provides a guide for teachers as they plan appropriate learning activities. Suggested term content and expected student outcomes are given for the six levels of the taxonomy to be introduced.

Whilst teachers may choose to vary the timing of instruction of different elements to suit their planning needs, it is expected that all identified learning outcomes will be achieved by the time the student completes the current year of schooling.

The teaching of the module is further supported by the inclusion of proformas, student worksheets and opinionaires that will assist in the recording of student learning outcomes, assessing levels of understanding and determining student attitudes towards the skill that has been taught. These may be photocopied for classroom use.

Other useful resources that will support the teaching of this strategy appear at the end of the module.

Skills for Explicit Teaching
Module 6
- Bloom's Taxonomy -

Term	Strategy	Student Learning Outcomes
1	**Remembering** **Understanding** **Applying**	**Students can:** • recall a definition; a sequenced list by time, order, importance and by acronym, • demonstrate understanding of concepts by translating ideas into their own words, or into graphic or visual form to • other everyday situations or tell how it may relate to other situations within the students experience.
2	**Analysing** **Evaluating** **Creating**	**Students can explain or demonstrate:** • how objects or situations are alike / different using physical and / or abstract attributes • how objects may be grouped, categorised or classified in relation to their attributes • that they can tell why they think something is the way that it is and can give judgements and support them • new products and ideas are generated through creative thinking
3	**The Integrated Taxonomy**	Students can explain that different types of thinking are required at each level of the taxonomy eg • Remembering questions require nothing more than memory, • Understanding - requires proof of understanding • Applying - explaining how something may fit into another known situation • Analysing requires breaking things into smaller parts to examine composition in close detail • Evaluating requires judgements and decision making • Creating requires original ideas that will produce something new, different or another way of looking at things.
4	**Student Project**	**Groups of students can:** • apply their understanding of the taxonomy in designing a unit of negotiated study through the development of questions and activities around the taxonomy

NOTE FOR TEACHERS: Teachers may choose to vary the content in any given school term. It is expected however that all children will be experienced in the use of all elements of the taxonomy described above and will have completed a unit of work based upon their own questions and activities using Blooms by the end of the current school year.

Background Information for Teachers
- Remembering Understanding Applying -

Often described as basic thinking skills, these three elements of **Bloom's taxonomy** provide the essential groundwork for the higher order thinking skills to be introduced later.
The table below indicates the types of questions, the nature of activities and possible student products for each of the first three levels of the newly revised taxonomy.

Level	Sample Questions Starters	Activities & Products
Remembering *Factual answers, recall and recognition.* List Name Describe Recount State	**Question starters at this level may include:** Label true or false... List the events as they happened. What evidence is there for... Tell how many... Tell about... Tell what happened next...	**Activities at this level may include:** Complete a timeline. Make an acrostic. Retell the story. **Student products at this level may include:** A list of information A facts chart. A story profile
Understanding *Translating, interpreting, showing understanding* Translate Outline Restate Interpret Summarise	**Question starters at this level may include:** In your own words... Tell the main idea... What is meant by...	**Activities at this level may include:** Summarise what happened when... Sequence the events. Retelling a story. **Student products at this level may include:** Cartoon strips Story maps Illustrations Play
Applying *Applying information gained in other (familiar) situations* Show how Illustrate Construct Use Complete	**Question starters at this level may include:** Tell about another time when... What could you ask about... What instructions could you give to...	**Activities at this level may include:** Construct a model Make a diorama Write a manual for... **Student products at this level may include:** A puzzle A game A model A map A set of instructions

Background Information for Teachers
- Analysing Evaluating Creating -

Often described as higher order thinking skills, these three elements of **Bloom's taxonomy** engage students in analytical, creative and critical thinking tasks.
The table below indicates the types of questions, the nature of activities and possible student products for each level of the newly revised taxonomy.

Level	Sample Questions Starters	Activities & Projects
Analysing *Break into parts to examine more closely* Compare Contrast Separate Distinguish	**Question starters at this level may include:** Explain similarities between… What things could not have occurred? What were the motives underlying… Separate the facts from the opinions in the story.	**Activities at this level may include:** Designing a questionnaire Making a jig-saw Depicting information graphically **Student products at this level may include:** Venn diagrams Compare/contrast charts Matrix charts Graphs
Evaluating *Judge, using criteria* Rank Substantiate Argue Validate Assess	**Question starters at this level may include:** Suggest a better reason for… Recommend some changes to… How effective is… What is your opinion of…	**Activities at this level may include:** Discussing issues Formulating arguments Writing critiques **Student products at this level may include:** Debates Rules Critical reviews Proposals Letter to the editor
Creating Combining information to new situations to create new products, ideas, etc. Create Invent Design Improve	**Question starters at this level may include:** Create a new character for the story. Invent a different way to… Find unusual uses for…	**Activities at this level may include:** Design a better… Find other ways to… Create an advertisement for… **Student products at this level may include:** Songs Books Magazines Inventions Ideas T.V. script Video production Unique ideas

Background Information for Teachers
- Integrated Taxonomy -

Using Bloom's Taxonomy In The Classroom

Using the six levels of Bloom's taxonomy to plan questions and activities provides the scope for student negotiation and the opportunity to differentiate the curriculum for some students in accordance with their interests, abilities and specific learning needs.

Teachers choosing to use the taxonomy in this way may structure learning experiences so that

- All students work through Remembering and Understanding stage, then select one activity from each of the other levels.

- All students work through Remembering and Understanding stage, then select activities from any other levels.

- Some work through Remembering and Understanding stage, others work at higher levels. (This will be particularly relevant for gifted students).

- All students select from any level.

- Some activities tagged essential, others as optional.

- Select a thinking process as a focus - eg Analysing (where instruction is being provided in that process).

- Some work through Remembering and Understanding stage, then write their own activity at preferred level.

- Students write their own questions from the taxonomy. (Engaging the students in this activity serves as a useful lead-in to the negotiated student project to follow.)

Bloom's taxonomy can be applied within a curriculum area or for a cross- curricula study of a theme or topic. As a planning tool, it can be used at all levels of schooling.

It can be also be used in conjunction with other thinking tools and strategies.

In the example on the following page, activities have been devised around 'Louise builds a house' by Louise Pfanner (a text in which the author makes her own thinking processes explicit as she designs a house to meet her needs and interests). Bloom's taxonomy is used to plan the activities for students as they respond to the text. In addition, activities that use the **Thinker's Keys** and **Six Hat Thinking** activities and match the appropriate level of the taxonomy are also presented.

This planning proforma makes explicit, the inter-relationship between each of the strategies and the nature of thinking involved across a range of tools.

A blank planning proforma that also includes the **Question Matrix** has been included for teachers wishing to integrate a number of thinking strategies as they plan teaching and learning activities.

An Integrated Approach To Planning, Teaching and Learning
Activities with a Thinking Skills Focus

Activities around a text -*'Louise builds a house'* by Louise Pfanner

	Blooms (Questions and Activities)	Thinker's Keys	Six Hat Thinking
Remembering (Factual answers recall and recognition.)	List the additions Louise made to her house. What were the jobs Louise had in the book? Name all the shapes making up the house.	**Alphabet -** List occupations A-Z List Buildings A-Z from the story? **Reverse -** List 10 things Louise did not build onto her house.	**White Hat** What facts can you remember
Understanding Translating, interpreting, showing understanding)	Make a collage depicting Louise's house. Retell the story in your own words. Create a story map for the important events in the story.	**Question key -** The answer is HOUSE. List 5 questions that can have only this answer?	**White Hat** What facts help us to establish what Louise may be like?
Applying (Using information gained in different, familiar situations)	Write an advertisement to sell the house in the real-estate section of the newspaper. Write a list of instructions showing the steps taken in building Louise's house. Make a pop-up page for the book showing the inside of Louise's house.	**Construction Key -** Build a model of your own house using junk materials.	**Blue Hat** What things would we need to think about before placing an advertisement in the paper?
Analysing (Break into parts to examine more closely)	Compare your house with the one in the story. Using information from the story, what do we know about Louise? Use SCUMPS to describe the house.	**Picture Key -** What could this represent in the story ★	**Red Hat** How did Louise and her sister feel when the house was finished? **Black Hat** What were some of the problems with the house?
Evaluating (Judge, use criteria, rank, substantiate)	What did you like and dislike about Louise's house? Explain. Draw your favourite part of the story and tell why you chose it. Should Louise have given her house to her sister? Why?	**What if key -** What if Louise were in a wheelchair? **Disadvantages key -** List disadvantages and then improvements to a watering can.	**Blue Hat** What could Louise build next? Say why you think your idea may be a good one. What might she need to think about first?
Creating (New products, ideas, etc.)	Design a house based on your own interests. Design a poster to show Louise's house. Write a poem about the ideal home.	**Combination key -** What things did Louise combine with a house? **Ridiculous -** Justify this statement - Everyone should build their own houses.	**Green Hat** Think of some creative ways in which the problems may have been solved.

Planning Proforma

For an integrated approach to planning teaching and learning activities with a thinking skills focus

	Blooms (Questions & Activities)	Thinker's Keys	Question Matrix	6 Hats/ Others
Remembering *(Factual answers, recall and recognition.)*		Alphabet - Reverse -	What is… Who is… Where is… How is… What can…	White Hat
Understanding *Translating, interpreting, showing understanding)*		Question Key -	Why did… How did… Where did… What did…	White Hat
Applying *(Using information gained in different, familiar situations)*		Construction Key -	How can… What can… Why can… Who can…	Blue Hat White Hat
Analysing *(Break into parts to examine more closely)*		Picture Key - Who would… Disadvantages Key -	What would… White Hat How would… Why would…	Red Hat SCUMPS
Evaluating *(Judge, use criteria, rank, substantiate)*		What if key - Interpretation Key - Disadvantages key	Which will… When will… Who will… How will…	Black Hat Yellow Hat Yellow Hat CAMPER
Creating *(New products, ideas, etc.)*		Combination Key - Inventions Key - Ridiculous - BAR -	What might… Why might… What will… When will…	Green Hat SCAMPER

Assessing and Recording Student Learning Outcomes
Module 6
Bloom's Taxonomy

Assessment of Student Outcomes

In order to assess the effectiveness of the explicit teaching of the skills of thinking, teachers will need to revisit the anticipated learning outcomes described at the beginning of this module. They may then choose to use some or all of the following means to assess the progress of individual students

- classroom observations
- anecdotal notes
- more formal (task-specific) achievement records
- evaluation of student products
- assessments of student attitudes

In order to assist teachers in designing suitable assessment activities, the following pages provide a range of proformas, worksheets and questionnaires that will assist in both the assessment and recording of student learning outcomes. The examples of student worksheets in this module have been designed to assess the understanding of upper primary age students.

Teacher's Note:
The examples that follow are designed to *assess and record* the student's understanding of the *thinking skill* that has just been taught, regardless of the curriculum content.

Teachers will need to employ other methods as suggested above when *reporting* the application of the skills to specific curriculum content, theme or topics taught.

Assessment of Student Learning
Class Record Sheet
Bloom's Taxonomy

Teacher's Note:

Revisit the student learning outcomes shown at the beginning of this module. Indicate level of student comprehension below. Indicate whether the student has

- been exposed to the content (EX)
- demonstrated mastery (M)

Add comments as required

Name of Student	Remembering Understanding Applying	Analysing Evaluating Creating	Integrated Taxonomy	Student Project	Comment

Student Worksheet 1

This year we have been answering questions and doing activities using **Bloom's Taxonomy**. Here are some questions that will help you show how well you understand the way the taxonomy works.

Can you draw a line to match the level of Bloom's Taxonomy with the statement that describes the type of questions found at each level? Have a try!!

This type of question shows that we understand.	**Remembering**
This type of question shows that we can apply what we know in other ways or show how something might be in another situation	**Understanding**
This type of question shows that we can make judgements or make decisions about things and explain the choices that we make.	**Applying**
This type of question shows that we can be creative and come up with new ideas	**Analysing**
This type of question shows that we remember.	**Evaluating**
This type of question shows that we can look at smaller parts of objects, events or situations.	**Creating**

Describe an activity that you have done this year that used all six levels of **Bloom's Taxonomy** in such a way that a visiting alien may be able to explain the way the taxonomy works to other aliens. (Use the back of this sheet if you run out of room.)

Student Worksheet 2

What do YOU think about... Bloom's Taxonomy?

What kinds of Bloom's Taxonomy activities do you like doing the most?
Explain why you feel this way.

What did you like the most about making up your own questions and activities using Bloom's.

If you had the chance to make up your project questions again, would this be better than if the teacher set all the questions? Explain your opinion.

Resources To Support This Module

Educational Impressions Inc. (1986)

Primary Topics 1 - create a centre about... series
Victoria: Hawker Brownlow Education

Bagley, M

Suppose the wolf were an octupus- books 1 & 2
Victoria: Hawker Brownlow Education

Dalton, J. (1985)

Adventures in thinking. Melbourne: Thomas Nelson.

Kelly, L. (1994)

Challenging minds. Victoria: Hawker Brownlow Education

Loveday, B. & Cannon, C. (1993)

The footbook for thinkers.(K-3 & 3-7) Melbourne: Longman Cheshire.

Victorian Department of Education. (1991)

Achieving excellence. Victoria: Directorate of School Education.

Thinking Skills For Explicit Teaching
Module 7
Planning, Decision-Making & Problem Solving

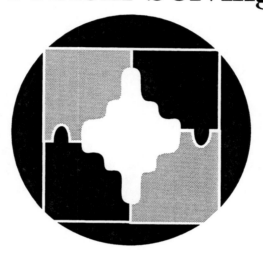

Introduction

It is suggested that teachers adopt a term-by-term approach to the teaching of **planning, decision-making and creative problem solving** culminating in a student-designed project around a negotiated topic.

The table on the next page provides a guide for teachers as they plan appropriate learning activities. Suggested term content and expected student outcomes are given for the thinking skills to be introduced.

While teachers may choose to vary the timing of instruction of different elements to suit their planning needs, it is expected that all identified learning outcomes will be achieved by the time the student completes the current year of schooling.

The teaching of the module is further supported by the inclusion of proformas, student worksheets and opinionaires that will assist in the recording of student learning outcomes, assessing levels of understanding and determining student attitudes towards the skill that has been taught. These may be photocopied for classroom use.

Other useful resources which will support the teaching of this strategy appear at the end of the module.

Skills For Explicit Teaching
Module 7
- Planning, Decision Making & Problem Solving -

Term	Strategy	Student Learning Outcomes
1	**Planning** **Decision Making**	**Students can:** • explain planning as a process that assists in organising thoughts and actions. • demonstrate an understanding of planning as a series of steps or sequential stages • can explain the process as a way to solve a problem or reach a goal
2	**Creative Problem Solving**	**Students can:** • explain and demonstrate the six stages of CPS as a method for systematically arriving at solutions • employ strategies introduced earlier (e.g. brainstorming, planning, decision-making)
3	**Action Planning**	**Students can:** • employ a range of methods, media and tech niques in developing a detailed plan of action for implementing solutions
4	**CPS Student Project**	**Students can:** • demonstrate previous learning in CPS and other thinking strategies through student-designed projects

Note:
Teachers may choose to teach creative problem solving through the Future Problem Solving process - for which there is an excellent coaching manual available -see resource list at the end of this module.

- Planning Processes -

Planning engages students in developing a series of steps that will result in reaching specific goals or objectives. Using planning processes assists students to understand the need to organise thinking in order to complete a task successfully, on time or within set constraints.
Planning promotes efficiency - it may save time, effort and/or money.

Some of the tools introduced in earlier modules can be used in the planning process, notably the **flow chart** (Module 5) and **Six-Hat Thinking** (Module 1).
Teachers choosing to use a **Six-Hat** strategy to introduce planning procedures may find the following sequence appropriate.

Hat	Questions To Ask...	Consider...
Blue Hat	Let's think about the planning task ahead of us - what do we need to consider?	Time restrictions Cost limits Where to start Materials required Likely steps involved
White Hat	What are the facts as we know them?	Establishing the boundaries of the task and resources available.
Green Hat	What is possible? Is there more than one way to reach the goal?	Listing a range of possible approaches that can achieve the objectives.
Yellow Hat	What are the positive aspects of each alternative?	Listing the relative strengths of each idea generated.
Black Hat	What are the limitations or difficulties with each alternative?	Listing the relative limitations of each idea generated.
Red Hat	How do we feel about each alternative? Which one do we feel will afford us the greatest chance of success?	Ranking alternatives according to appropriate criteria. Deciding on a preferred line of action.

In providing students with opportunities to practise planning skills, students engage in planning tasks such as

- an end-of-year production
- an end-of-term celebration
- class fund raising events
- a video production

- a practical demonstration
- an experiment
- a negotiated project
- a lesson presentation

– Decision Making –

Decision making engages students in critical thinking as alternatives are considered, priorities assigned and plans are actioned.

Using a decision-making model during the planning stages of a project will assist students in making the most appropriate choices before tasks are undertaken.

Teachers introducing decision-making may choose to use the model adapted from Parks & Black (1993) presented below.

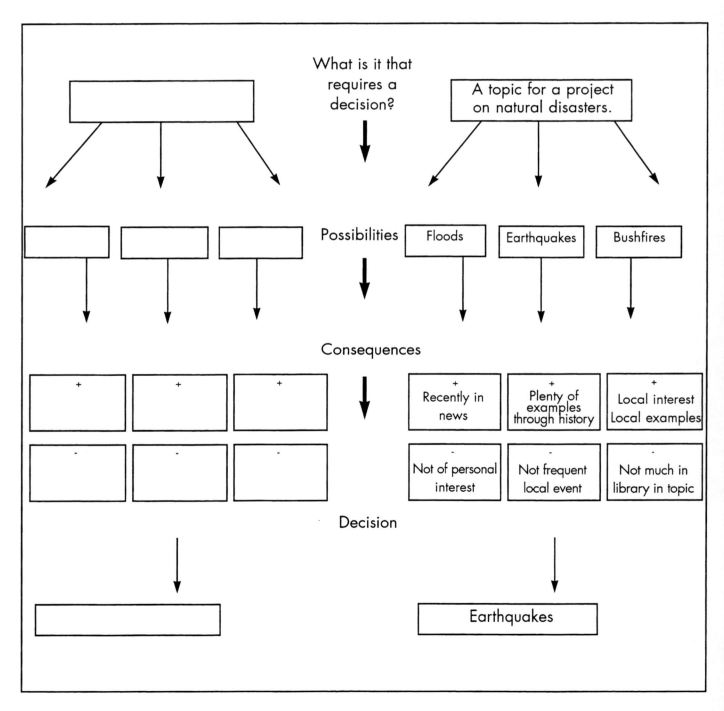

What is it that requires a decision? → A topic for a project on natural disasters.

Possibilities → Floods | Earthquakes | Bushfires

Consequences

+ Recently in news	+ Plenty of examples through history	+ Local interest Local examples
- Not of personal interest	- Not frequent local event	- Not much in library in topic

Decision → Earthquakes

- Creative Problem Solving -

Creative problem solving (CPS) engages students in the higher order thinking skills of analytical, critical and creative thinking through a six-step process that provides a preferred solution to an underlying problem.

'Be a problem solver' by Bob Eberle and Bob Standish (1990) contains many introductory activities suitable for the middle -upper primary years. Their CPS is described as a method of arriving at solutions which requires collaborative brainstorming at each of the six steps described below.

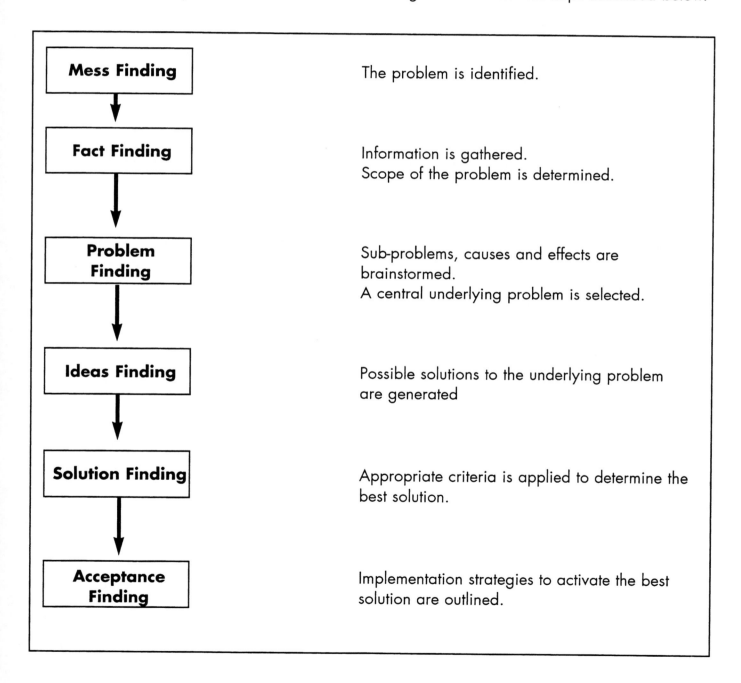

Mess Finding	The problem is identified.
Fact Finding	Information is gathered. Scope of the problem is determined.
Problem Finding	Sub-problems, causes and effects are brainstormed. A central underlying problem is selected.
Ideas Finding	Possible solutions to the underlying problem are generated
Solution Finding	Appropriate criteria is applied to determine the best solution.
Acceptance Finding	Implementation strategies to activate the best solution are outlined.

- Action Planning -

Who?   **What?**   **When?**   **Where?**   **How?**   **Why?**

Students engaged in action planning employ a range of methods, media and techniques in developing a detailed plan for implementing solutions identified through the Creative Problem Solving process.

Action plans usually detail

> - **WHO** will do **WHAT**
> - **WHEN** and **WHERE** solutions will be activated
> - **HOW** and **WHY** the solution will work.

All steps to a successful outcome are elaborated upon, timelines set and resource needs determined and allocated.

Action plans are often presented as a matrix table or flow chart (see Module 5).
However, Eberle & Standish (1990) suggest students demonstrate a creative approach to action planning. Instead of a written plan, teachers may offer students opportunities to

- explain the plan using a storyboard or cartoon sketches
- act out problems and solutions using role play or puppets
- present demonstrations of models or constructions that form part of the solution
- create an illustrated manual
- produce an interpretative dance or mime
- produce a video that presents a visual presentation of the plan
- write a newspaper article or letter to the editor
- devise an alternative presentation negotiated with students.

Assessing and Recording Student Learning Outcomes
Module 7
Planning, Decision Making & Problem Solving

Assessment Of Student Outcomes

In order to assess the effectiveness of the explicit teaching of the skills of thinking, teachers will need to revisit the anticipated learning outcomes described at the beginning of this module. They may then choose to use some of all or the following means to assess the progress of individual students

- classroom observations
- anecdotal notes
- more formal (task- specific) achievement records
- evaluation of student products
- assessments of student attitudes

In order to assist teachers in designing suitable assessment activities, the following pages provide a range of proformas, worksheets and questionnaires which will assist in both the assessment and recording of student learning outcomes. The examples of student worksheets in this module have been designed to assess the understanding of upper primary age students.

Note :
The examples that follow are designed to assess and record the student's understanding of the thinking skill that has just been taught, regardless of the curriculum content.

Teachers will need to employ other methods as suggested above when reporting the application of the skills to specific curriculum content, theme or topics taught.

Class Record Sheet
Planning, Decision Making & Problem Solving

Note:

Revisit the student learning outcomes shown at the beginning of this module. Indicate level of student comprehension below. Indicate whether the student has

- been exposed to the content (EX)
- demonstrated mastery (M)

Add comments as required

Name of Student	Planning	Decision Making	Creative Problem Solving	CPS Student Project	Comment

Student Worksheet 1

Here are some activities about CPS that will show others how well you understand it.

Creative Problem Solving	
1. Write the six steps involved in creative problem solving in the boxes below. Check that you have them in the correct order.	2. Explain what is meant by 'action planning' by describing an action plan that you have created as part of a classroom activity this year. Include a discussion of the decision making processes that you used.

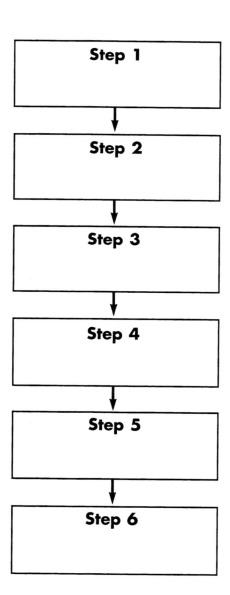

Step 1

Step 2

Step 3

Step 4

Step 5

Step 6

Student Worksheet 2

What do YOU think about ....Creative Problem Solving?

Do you think that CPS is a good way of coming up with possible solutions to problems? Explain why you feel this way.

What did you like the most about your own creative problem solving project?

How would you feel if you had the chance to use CPS again as a classroom activity? Explain your opinion.

How might you use the CPS process, a decision making model or action planning to solve problems when you are older and have left school? Try to give more than one example.

Module Support Resources

Dalton, J.(1990)   *Adventures in thinking.* Melbourne: Thomas Nelson.

Eberle, B & Standish, B. (1990)   *Be a problem Solver.* Victoria:
                                     Hawker Brownlow Education

Future Problem Solving Program (1994)   *FPS Coaching manual.* Victoria: Future Problem
                                     Solving Program.

Parks, S. &   *Organising thinking - graphic organisers.*
Black, H. (1990)   Victoria: Hawker Brownlow Education.

The Explicit Teaching of Thinking Skills
- A Whole School Approach -

Although the modules may be used in isolation or in an order different to that presented, both content and complexity increase from the first module to the last.

Each module has been designed to build upon the concepts introduced earlier and many of the modules revisit strategies encountered in previous modules. This has the effect of reinforcing student learning and establishing links between tools and strategies.

Primary schools with a R-7 student population may find it appropriate to use the modules in the sequence presented in this book.

Primary schools with a K-6 student population will choose to either

- select one module to be omitted from the sequence
- integrate the content of one of the modules across other year levels so that the total content presented in this book is still covered by all students in the course of their primary schooling.

Module 5 may prove to be the most appropriate module to consider if the second option above is selected. In this case, the graphic organisers would be introduced during the last two years of primary school - to compliment the introduction of Bloom's taxonomy and the problem solving processes.

A suggested scope and sequence for both R-7 and K-6 schools appears on the next page. Following this, a summary of analytical, critical, and creative thinking skills has been tabulated for the benefit of schools wishing to introduce additional skills for thinking.
The table provides a suggested entry level for each skill. This should be treated as a guide only.

A R–7 Scope Sequence

Thinking Strategy For Explicit Teaching	Year Level	Instruction Focus
Six Hat Thinking	R-1	6 Hats – introduced one at a time and 3 simple hat sequences, including • Evaluation sequence • Caution sequence • Design sequence
Extended Brainstorming	Year 2	4 elements of brainstorming, including • Fluency • Flexibility • Originality • Elaboration
Questioning Techniques	Year 3	A range of question types i.e. • Open and closed questions • Fat and skinny questions • Student self-generated questions
Thinker's Keys	Year 4	A ranhe of keys to promote different thinking, including Alphabet Disadvantages Reverse Key What if … BAR Construction Picture Question Key
Graphic Organisers	Year 5	A range of ways of organising thinking and information, including Concept mapping Venn diagrams Fishbone Simple webbing The matrix Flow charts Mind maps Consequence Wheel
Bloom's Taxonomy	Year 6	A range of higher and lower order questions, including • Remembering/Understanding/Applying • Analysing • Evaluating • Creating
Creative Problem Solving	Year 7	Strategies that integrate many of the strategies previously taught, including Decision making CPS Process Action planning

A K-6 Scope Sequence

Thinking Strategy For Explicit Teaching	Year Level	Instruction Focus
Six Hat Thinking	K–1	6 hats – introduced one at a time simple hat sequences, including • Evaluation sequence • Caution sequence • Design sequence
Extended Brainstorming	Year 2	4 elements of brainstorming, including • Fluency • Flexibility • Originality • Elaboration
Questioning Techniques	Year 3	A range of question types i.e. • Open and closed questions • Fat and skinny questions • ICE questions
Thinker's Keys	Year 4	A range of keys to promote different thinking, including Alphabet　　Disadvantages　BAR Reverse Key　What if…　　　Construction Picture Question Key
Bloom's Taxonomy	Year 5	A range of higher and lower order questions, including • Remembering/Understanding/Applying • Analysing • Evaluating • Creating
Graphic Organisers		A range of ways of organising thinking and information, including Concept mapping　　Venn diagrams Fishbone　　　　　Simple webbing
Creative Problem Solving	Year 6	Strategies that integrate many of the strategies previously taught, including Decision making, CPS Process Action planning
Graphic Organisers		A range of ways of organising thinking and information, including The Matrix Flow Charts Mind maps Consequence Wheel

Schools designing their own scope and sequence for explicit teaching of thinking skills which goes beyond the strategies introduced in this book may find the following tables useful in guiding decision-making.

▓ Denotes suitable for use at this level

← Denotes suitable for possible introduction at this level, particularly for gifted students

Creative Thinking Skill	P	1	2	3	4	5	6	7
Fluency	▓	▓	▓	▓	▓	▓	▓	▓
Flexibility			▓	▓	▓	▓	▓	▓
Originality			←	▓	▓	▓	▓	▓
Elaboration			←	▓	▓	▓	▓	▓

Brainstorming (Affective)	P	1	2	3	4	5	6	7
Brainstorming (Affective)			←	▓	▓	▓	▓	▓

Creative Problem Solving	P	1	2	3	4	5	6	7
Creative Problem Solving Tools - CPS, Future Problem Solving								▓

Cort Thinking	P	1	2	3	4	5	6	7
Cort Thinking								
Random input (CoRT 4)			▓	▓	▓	▓	▓	▓
Stepping Stones (CoRT 4)			▓	▓	▓	▓	▓	▓
Dominant Idea (CoRT 4)				▓	▓	▓	▓	▓
Yes, No, Po (CoRT 4)					▓	▓	▓	▓
Remove the faults (CoRT 4)					▓	▓	▓	▓

Six Thinking Hats	P	1	2	3	4	5	6	7
Six Thinking Hats	One at a ←	hat time	▓	▓	▓	▓	▓	▓

Think Lanes	P	1	2	3	4	5	6	7
Think Lanes	▓	▓	▓	▓	▓	▓	▓	▓

Analytical and Critical Thinking Skill	P	1	2	3	4	5	6	7
Analogies					▓	▓	▓	▓
Bloom's Analysis							▓	▓
Bloom's Evaluation							▓	▓
Cort Thinking	▓	▓	▓	▓	▓	▓	▓	▓
P.M.I. (CoRT 1)			▓	▓	▓	▓	▓	▓
C.A.F. (CoRT 1)					▓	▓	▓	▓
C&S (CoRT 1)					▓	▓	▓	▓
CoRT 3 series					▓	▓	▓	▓
Evaluation (CoRT 4)					▓	▓	▓	▓
Analytical Tools								
Venn diagrams, Concept Maps, Webs, The Grid					▓	▓	▓	▓
Consequence wheel, fish bone, Pie chart					▓	▓	▓	▓
Reasoning (Inductive)				▓	▓	▓	▓	▓
Reasoning (Deductive)				▓	▓	▓	▓	▓
Hypothesising	▓	▓	▓	▓	▓	▓	▓	▓
Planning (Ago, Apc, Opv, from CoRT 1)				▓	▓	▓	▓	▓
Prioritising				▓	▓	▓	▓	▓
Questioning								
Fat & Skinny Questions				▓	▓	▓	▓	▓
Student generated questions				▓	▓	▓	▓	▓
Sequencing Tools – Flow charts, Timelines, The Frame, Sequence charts						▓	▓	▓
Philosophical Inquiry							▓	▓

Combined Skills - Thinking Keys	P	1	2	3	4	5	6	7
Reverse Listing							▓	▓
What if...	▓	▓	▓	▓	▓	▓	▓	▓
Disadvantages				▓	▓	▓	▓	▓
Combination			▓	▓	▓	▓	▓	▓
Bar (& Scamper)		←	▓	▓	▓	▓	▓	▓
Alphabet		▓	▓	▓	▓	▓	▓	▓
Variations	▓	▓	▓	▓	▓	▓	▓	▓
Picture	▓	▓	▓	▓	▓	▓	▓	▓
Prediction				▓	▓	▓	▓	▓
Different Uses				▓	▓	▓	▓	▓
Ridiculous		▓	▓	▓	▓	▓	▓	▓
Commonality				▓	▓	▓	▓	▓
Question			▓	▓	▓	▓	▓	▓
Brainstorming	▓	▓	▓	▓	▓	▓	▓	▓
Inventions			▓	▓	▓	▓	▓	▓
Remove the Fault					▓	▓	▓	▓
Brick Wall							▓	▓
Construction	▓	▓	▓	▓	▓	▓	▓	▓
Forced Relationships			←		▓	▓	▓	▓
Alternatives	▓	▓	▓	▓	▓	▓	▓	▓
Interpretation					▓	▓	▓	▓

A Word In Closing

It is worthwhile to emphasise two main points stressed throughout this book.

Firstly, the framing of models and strategies into a sequence for explicit teaching at specific year levels will provide opportunities for all students to become familiar with the tools for thinking in a systematic fashion. This is an empowering process - effective instruction will provide every student with everlasting skills - the tools for life-long learning.

Secondly, it is important to re-emphasise that the sequencing of thinking skills for classroom instruction does not preclude teachers from using tools or strategies outside of their particular year level in their own planning and programming of teaching and learning activities. It is appropriate for teachers to draw upon the tools and strategies that they prefer and can employ effectively in the course of their every day teaching. What is important, however, is that 'old favourites' are not taught at the exclusion of other methods.

Adherence to a whole - school scope and sequence will ensure that this cannot occur.

Good thinking !

References

Resources listed here represent those that have been cited within the modules or have had a major influence in shaping the content of this book.

Bagley, M — *Suppose the wolf were an octopus- books 1 & 2* Victoria: Hawker Brownlow Education

Bellanca, J. & Fogarty, R. (1989) — *Patterns for thinking, patterns for transfer.* Victoria: Hawker Brownlow Education

Bellanca, J. & Fogarty, R. (1991) — *Blueprints for thinking in the cooperative classroom.* Victoria: Hawker Brownlow Education.

Black, H. et. al. (1992) — *Tracks - pathways for gifted children.* Cammeray, NSW: Martin Education

de Bono, E. (1992) — *Six thinking hats for schools. Books1-4* Victoria: Hawker Brownlow Education

Buzan, T. (1995) — *The mind map book.* London: BBC Books

Dalton, J. (1990) — *Adventures in Thinking.* South Melbourne: Thomas Nelson.

Dickinson ,et.al. (1987) — *Brainstorming - activities for creative thinking.* Sunnyvale, CA: Creative Publications.

Eberle, B & Standish, B. (1990) — *Be a problem Solver.* Victoria: Hawker Brownlow Education

Fligor, M. (1993) — *Brainstorming - the book of topics.* Victoria: Hawker Brownlow Education.

Fogarty,R. & Belanca.J. (1989) — *Patterns for thinking - patterns for transfer* Palatine, IL: Skylight Publishing.

Future Problem Solving Program (1994) — *FPS Coaching manual.* Victoria: Future Problem Solving Program.

Langrehr, J.(1993) — *Better questions, better thinking. Books 1 &2.* Sydney: Longman Cheshire.

Langrehr, J.(1994) — *Become a better thinker.* North Brighton Victoria:Wrightbooks

Langrehr, J.(1996) — *Thinking chips for thinking students.* Victoria:Hawker Brownlow Education.

Margulies, N. (1992) — *Mapping inner space.* Victoria: Hawker Brownlow Education

Parks, S. & Black, H. (1990) — *Organising thinking - graphic organisers. Books I & II.* Victoria: Hawker Brownlow Education.

Ryan T. (1990) — *Thinker's keys for kids.* Woodridge, Qld:Logan West School Support Centre

Wiederhold,C.(1991) — *Co-operative learning and critical thinking. The question matrix.* San Juan Capistrano, CA: Resources for Teachers